Meeting with your Master in the Morning

Meeting with your Master in the Morning

to meet with His world throughout the day.

ELIZABETH ROBLES

iUniverse, Inc.
New York Bloomington

Meeting with your Master in the Morning
to meet with His world throughout the day.

iUniverse books may be ordered through booksellers or by contacting:

iUniverse
1663 Liberty Drive
Bloomington, IN 47403
www.iuniverse.com
1-800-Authors (1-800-288-4677)

Because of the dynamic nature of the Internet, any Web addresses or links contained in this book may have changed since publication and may no longer be valid. The views expressed in this work are solely those of the author and do not necessarily reflect the views of the publisher, and the publisher hereby disclaims any responsibility for them.

ISBN: 978-1-4502-0483-5 (pbk)
ISBN: 978-1-4502-0482-8 (ebook)

Library of Congress Control Number: 2009914205

Printed in the United States of America

iUniverse rev. date: 1/21/10

Acknowledgements

I want to thank the Lord Jesus Christ for the "Meetings in the Morning" that have helped me along life's journey. I thank you for the incredible privilege of knowing You and for the honor it is to serve You. I am eternally grateful.

Virginia Wilson, thank you for making the time to edit this book and for your words of encouragement. I owe you a box of green markers.

Mike Marsh and Rod Williamson of Digital Press, thank you for the beautiful design for the book. Thank you for your hard work and for your promptness in getting the first copies with such short notice.

For those who attend An Evening in the Word monthly meetings, Thank you for your prayers, support, and for your love. You are special and I am honored to call you friends.

Forward

Meeting with the Master in the morning is a collection of sixty devotions written to bring encouragement, hope, comfort, and strength.

In our day-to-day journey, we are often bombarded with different problems and heartaches. It's what we call life. Life is not always fair and sometimes we carry the scars of its assaults.

Meeting with the Master was written with the hope that as you spend time with your Master in the morning, you will be strengthened and energized by His Spirit and that you will feel confident to face the world. Regardless of where you are in your spiritual journey, you will be blessed as you allow the Word of God to bring hope and courage as you travel throughout the day in His world.

These devotions were written from my personal "meetings with the Master."

I pray that you will walk away with a renewed hope and a joy that bubbles over into your day. May His Holy Spirit refresh you and restore to you gladness and joy.

Elizabeth Robles

Day One

Establish my steps and direct them by [means of] Your
word; let not any iniquity have dominion over me.

Psalm 119:133 Amplified

The book of Genesis records for us that Noah was a righteous man, blameless among the people of his time and he walked with God. (Gen.6:9) Noah was a man that understood that being real was not the most important thing but *being right with God was the most important thing.* That still holds true today. Everyone else was doing all sorts of evil but Noah was blameless. While others made a choice to follow in the footsteps of Cain's rebellion and run from God, Noah walked with God. Noah's attitude seemed to be so confident that he considered the world to have gone crazy. He believed he was the only one in his right mind. That is confidence! Where did this confidence come from? I believe that Noah was confident because he had learned to listen to God. As he walked with His God, he became more in tune with His voice. He learned that God's voice would direct his steps.

God's voice would show him how to walk in a world that had lost its perspective and was doing evil. Our world today is no different. Evil is everywhere and man still wants to do what is right in his own sight. So many voices scream and tell us what we should believe and do. They tell us how to conform to this world.

But, God is looking for those who will listen to His voice and walk so closely to Him, that even when He whispers, he will be heard. He is looking for men and women who will not be conformed to the patterns of this world but will be transformed by the renewing of their minds. He is looking for men and women who will choose to do what is right and just, *even* when it is not the popular thing to do.

In the same manner, that Noah listened to God as he walked with Him, so God wants you and me to listen to His voice. He wants us to cultivate an awareness of His presence in our lives. God speaks to you and me every day. One way He speaks is through His word. His word is alive, active and full of energizing power. His word gives direction, encouragement, hope, and reminds us daily of His love and promises.

Listening to God's voice is not always an easy thing to do but it is a necessary thing for every follower of Jesus Christ.

Are you a good listener?

Don't let the world around you squeeze you into its own mould, but let God re-make you so that your whole attitude of mind is changed. Romans 12:2 (New Testament in Modern English: J.B.Phillips)

Day Two

O Lord, our Lord, How majestic is thy name in all the earth, who hast displayed Thy splendor above the heavens!

Psalm 8:1 NASB

Praise is what we were created to do. We praise God for His deeds and we worship Him for who He is. We praise Him for His character and His glory. Praise is magnifying God and worshipping Him. Worship literally means to "kiss." It is used when giving homage, reverence, and veneration to someone or something. However, worship is more than singing and giving thanks. Worship also involves action that recognizes God for His nature and attributes.

God made you with the ability to praise Him. The question is not whether you and I will praise and worship Him, but rather, HOW to praise and worship Him. God demands total adoration from His children. Those of us that are called by His name are to worship only Him. Man has often been guilty of worshipping his career, his family, material possessions, etc. Scripture teaches that a man or woman is a servant to what he worships. Worship and serving go hand in hand. They cannot be separated. Read Matthew 4:18-20 to see this truth.

When you and I begin to praise God, we open the door to His courts, giving God the opportunity to pour out His blessings over our lives. Praise invites His miraculous acts on our behalf. What an incredible thought! When I use my mouth to praise and worship the One who created me, He is moved to bless me. Praise is what we do because our hearts cannot hold back the adoration that is rightfully His.

We praise Him regardless of the situations or circumstances.

We praise Him in the storm and in the calmness.

We praise Him in the valley and on the mountaintop.

We praise Him when we are employed and unemployed.

We praise Him when our bodies are sick and when our bodies are whole.

We praise Him when our pockets are full and when they are empty.

We praise Him because He and He alone is worthy of all our praise!

Check your praise-o-meter? Are you praising Him regardless and in spite of where you are today?

O God, how majestic You are. You are worthy of all glory and honor and praise. There is no other God like You. You are faithful and holy. You are righteous and just. You are all knowing and all powerful. You are the redeemer and giver of life. You are joy and peace. You are strong and mighty. Fill my heart with praise and my mouth with a new song. I choose to proclaim Your goodness, not just for what you do, but for Who You are! In Jesus' Name.

Day Three

Be anxious for nothing, but in everything by prayer and supplication, with thanksgiving, let your requests be made known to God; and the peace of God, which surpasses all understanding, will guard your hearts and minds through Christ Jesus.

Philippians 4:6-7 NKJV

God's plans for your life are good (Jer. 29:11), His plans are to give you a hope and a peace beyond human understanding. You may and probably will go through difficult times but He has promised to build "good" into your life, (Rom.8:28).

Satan will tell you to worry but God says the opposite. He says TRUST ME. It is in trusting Him that we can have an unshakeable peace and walk with the assurance of His promises on a daily basis.

Is it really possible to gain and maintain the true peace of God? YES and YES!

Recognize your dependence on God. A heart that can find its identity in Christ is a heart of peace. When you and I rush in trying to solve our own problems in our own strength, we become people of worry and strife. Take responsibility for your own actions *but* let God have the reins to your life.

<u>Pray always.</u> The enemy is paralyzed and cannot defeat you when you are on your spiritual knees. Prayer keeps you focused on the Lord and His strength rather than focusing on the problem.

<u>Trust God.</u> When thoughts of fear begin to invade your mind, tell the Lord what you are feeling. Fear empowers the enemy *but* trust is the best repellent to use against fear. Ask the Lord to strengthen your faith and to help you trust Him more.

<u>Focus only On God.</u> Let go of all negative thoughts and release negativity from your life. Let your heart be focused on God and His Word and all He can do and yearns to do for you. God sees tremendous potential in you and He will grow your faith and trust in Him.

Father, I know that You have good plans for my life, help me to learn to walk in Your peace regardless of the storms of life that toss me to and fro. I want to have an unshakeable confidence in You. I want to speak the words of life over my situations instead of negative words that discourage and destroy. Therefore, I choose to let go of fear and negativity and I pick up Your Word, which teaches me to how walk in perfect confidence and trust. In Jesus name.

Day Four

The words of the Lord are pure words; as silver tried in a furnace on the earth, refined seven times.

Psalm 12:6 NASB

I love God's Word! There is no other book that has brought life and transformation into my heart as His Word. It is the only book that can be read that provides fresh revelation and treasure every time you read within its pages. His Word brings hope, direction for life, wisdom, assurance of your salvation, and comfort in times of need. The key to finding our hope and strength in His Word is to KNOW it. It isn't enough to have it as a decoration on our tables, but it must be opened daily and read with the guidance of the Holy Spirit. It must be studied. It must be hidden in your heart and in mine. The Holy Spirit will bring refreshing to our souls as He guides us through God's Word.

The Holy Spirit will quicken God's Word in our hearts and will make it come alive.

God's Word will encourage you and strengthen you. It will transform your life. His Word will sustain you as you go through the valley. You will find your victory in His promises that are written for you in His Word.

There are many books, many good and informative books to read *but* there is only one GOD BOOK. Devour His Word and daily enjoy the blessings He has *just for you*.

This book will either keep you from sin or sin will keep you from this book. D.L.Moody

Day Five

He that dwelleth in the secret place of the most High shall
abide under the shadow of the Almighty.

Psalm 91:1 KJV

The word "abide" means to lodge or set up camp. Let's read it again: He that dwells in the secret place of the most High shall lodge under the shadow of the Almighty. A shadow is not seen but it is always there. So to be in somebody's shadow would require closeness to that person. To be able to lodge under God's shadow requires a closeness that is beyond the norm.

How do I get this close to God? Is it by going to church? No, going to church is good and Scripture teaches that we should gather together. However the Bible does not teach "draw near to church and you'll be close to God." The Word teaches, "Draw near to God and He will draw near to you." (James 5:8)

The depth of your relationship with God depends on the time you spend with Him. You spend time with <u>whom you love</u> *and* <u>with whom you are in love.</u>

Are you a person that spends time with God, loving on Him and enjoying His presence? Do you find yourself talking to Him throughout the day? Do you catch yourself throwing little arrows of love His way? If your answer is yes, then you are reaching a place of abiding under His shadow. That is definitely the best place to be. Under His shadow, you enjoy closeness to the Father that is unlike that of *just* being a son or daughter. You are so close, you can hear Him speak.

Under His shadow- you will find refuge.

Under His shadow- you will find strength.

Under His shadow- you will find healing.

Under His shadow- you will find comfort.

Under His shadow- you will find peace and joy.

Go ahead, rest and set up camp under His shadow. There is no better place to be!

Father, my heart echoes the words of David; "As the deer pants for the water brooks, so my soul pants for You. My soul thirsts for God, for the living God." I want to rest securely under the shadow of your wings. I don't want to lodge anywhere else. I purpose to seek You with my whole heart and I will pursue You with passion and intent. In Jesus' name.

Day Six

Jesus said to them, "I most positively say to you, before Abraham was born I AM.

John 8:58 Power NT

I AM encompasses all that Jesus is and all His character and attributes. God is not I was or I will be *but* He is the great I AM. In Exodus 3:13-15, He sent Moses with the message, tell them *I AM* has sent you.

Let me ask you, today, who do you need Jesus to be? If you only see Him as your Savior, in all probability that is all He will be to you. But He desires to be so much more.

I AM is peace- in the craziness of the day- He speaks peace to your heart.

I AM is wisdom- when confused and unsure what steps to take- He is your wisdom.

I AM is healing- when the body is wracked with pain and it seems hopeless- He is your healer.

I AM is friend- when you feel alone and friendless- He is One who sticks closer than a brother; who will never abandon you.

I AM is your shepherd- when you have lost your way in life- He leaves the flock to find you.

I AM is strength- when you feel drained and empty- He is your strength.

I AM is provider- when there is lack- He supplies your needs.

I AM is sustainer- when you can't take another step- He carries you and sustains you with His mighty right arm.

I AM is freedom- when the worries of this life have entangled you- He is your liberator and freedom.

I AM is joy- in your sadness and despair- He is your joy, the glory and the lifter of your head.

I AM is Lord-He is your Lord Who will lead you. He will make a dry place in the midst of the river and He will cause a river to flow in the dry place. He will take you over the hurdles of life and you will be victorious.

Who is He? He is the great *I AM*! He is your faithful Lord who will never leave you nor forsake you. Jesus is always with you!

One of the marks of spiritual maturity is the quiet confidence that God is in control- without the need to understand why He does what He does. Anonymous

Day Seven

… The Lord said to Gideon, "With the three hundred men
that lapped I will save you and give the Midianites into
your hands…"

Judges 7:1-7 NIV

Have you ever felt like your back was up against a wall and there was
no way out? I must be honest and tell you that I have felt like that and
I have never liked that feeling.

Many times when we find ourselves in this predicament, we have the
tendency to point our finger at the world, or Satan and blame them for
the difficulty in our lives.

Will you allow me to point out a truth that is often overlooked?

That truth that we often fail to recognize is that God may be the One
who is orchestrating our challenging time.

I know you're probably reading this and thinking- *no way*. God is my
protector and He wouldn't do this to me. He wouldn't allow me to go
through this. But maybe God is trying to get your attention. Time and
again in Scripture, we see the Lord use difficulties to build faith. It is
so easy to trust God when everything is going smoothly and in our
favor. But there are times that God may remove those comforts in our

lives. He may remove those things that give us a false sense of security to remind us that He and He alone is our true source of strength and security.

Read today's verses carefully and you will notice that three times God downsized Gideon's Army. It dwindled from 32,000 men to 300 soldiers. I don't know about you but if I were in that Army, 32,000 men makes more sense than 300. It would certainly be more comfortable and give a greater confidence that the enemy would be defeated. In our finite minds, we say, that is not the way to win a war. No one goes to battle to lose.

300 soldiers cannot do it. You might be right, but remember, the Lord is on their side. "With God all things are possible." You and God make a majority. "If God is for you, who can be against you?" God is more than able to get us from the place of feeling totally overwhelmed by our problems to the place where we sense His overwhelming peace and strength.

So when things have your back against the wall don't think you have been forgotten or forsaken. There is no way that could ever happen! You are always on His mind and in His heart.

The things you and I have prized: friends, finances, and successes may vanish but it's really okay. That's not what wins the battles of life. He does!

Stand your ground and keep your eyes on Jesus!

The Devil is not terribly frightened by our human effort and credentials. But he knows his kingdom will be damaged when we begin to lift up our hearts to God.

Jim Cymbala

Day Eight

Casting the whole of your care {all your anxieties, all your worries, all your concerns, once and for all} on Him, for He cares for you affectionately and cares about you watchfully.

1 Peter 5:7 Amplified

The Father knows that it is in our daily lives that we often become anxious and restless. Waiting on that doctor's report, waiting for that job offer, waiting for that breakthrough. All this leads us to become anxious and it causes us to feel stressed and sometimes fearful. What if that report is bad, what if I don't get that job, what if my breakthrough doesn't come?

The "what ifs" of life can keep us in a frenzy- if we let them.

Carrying the worries and stresses of life in your own strength can indicate that you have not fully trusted God with your life.

You and I must come to the place in our walk with the Master that we understand that He cares for us. This requires humility of heart. God wants us to admit our need and then He wants us to trust Him to take care of us.

If we have sinned and this is the reason we are struggling; He waits for us to repent. Then He can comes alongside to be our Helper. He still cares and He still helps.

Letting God have your cares requires action. "Cast all your cares on Him for He cares for you." Don't be passive and wallow in self-pity. He loves you and is calling to you, "Come over here and let me strengthen you and let me refresh you."

Day Nine

…But the Comforter, the Holy Spirit, whom the Father will send in My name, that One will teach you all things and will remind you of everything which I Myself said to you.

John 14:26 Power NT

The Holy Spirit is not an *it*- He is the third person of the Trinity.

The Holy Spirit takes residence in your heart and He comforts, guides, teaches, and prays for you. In those moments of despair and woundedness, the Holy Spirit brings comfort.

In those moments of discouragement- He encourages and fills your heart with joy and peace.

In those moments when you cannot understand- He is wisdom and guidance.

In those moments when you cannot pray- it is He who intercedes on your behalf. (Rom 8:26) He speaks on your behalf. What a thought. The Holy Spirit is not only aware of your heart and need, *but* He knows the mind and will of the Father. He is able to form that perfect prayer on your behalf.

The Holy Spirit has also come to lead you into a life of prayer. I don't know about you but sometimes I can become very confused about prayer. I can make it seem so complicated. If you go to any bookstore, you will find countless books on the subject of prayer. Some of the books will have detailed formulas on how you are to pray. There can be so many theories and questions regarding this great privilege and ministry that it can leave one baffled. It can cause us to become discouraged to the point where we even stop praying. But the Holy Spirit Who dwells in you and me is desirous of keeping us close to the Father's heart through prayer.

Let me share a few powerful ways the Spirit helps you in your prayers:

1. In prayer the Holy Spirit manifests the presence of Christ in you.

2. In prayer the Holy Spirit seals God's promise in your heart.

3. In prayer the comforter speaks hope to you.

4. In prayer the Holy Spirit releases His rivers of peace, joy, and love into your heart and soul.

True prayer is God the Holy Spirit praying to God the Father in the name of God the Son, and the believer's heart is the prayer room.

Anonymous

Day Ten

Who is like Thee among the gods, O Lord? Who is like Thee
majestic in holiness, awesome in praises, working wonders?

Exodus 15:11 KJV

Did you know that our mouths are the vehicles by which we can use the
weapons of warfare? God's weapons are used by means of the mouth:
proclaiming, declaring, prophesying, praising, worshipping, and confessing. Your mouth has power to speak words of life or words of death.
What are you speaking to your situations? Are you confessing what you
see or are you confessing what God's Word says?

David destroyed Goliath because he refused to listen to what others
said and instead exalted and praised God. This got him "a-head."

Jehosophat saw victory because the people began to praise God. He
knew the importance of praise and sent the worshippers in front. What
if every military organization sent the choirs ahead to prepare the at-
mosphere for battle? Every war just might be shorter and less costly.

Paul and Silas were freed from their prison chains because they prayed
and sang praises to God. If anyone had a reason to feel sorry, it was
these two. They had been thrown to the lowest part of the prison, and
were surrounded by stench and rats. But they refused to give in to their
circumstances and chose to worship the One true God instead!

(Put your name here) triumphs as she/he prays and praises God!

God, I want my words to be in agreement with Your Word. I want to be a praiser and a pray-er and declare the good works of God. Set a watchman over my mouth and a guard over my lips and help me to speak words of encouragement. In Jesus' Name.

Day Eleven

Delight yourself in the Lord and He will give you the desires of your heart. Commit your way to the Lord; trust in Him and He will do this:

Psalm 37:4-5 NIV

When you and I are living our lives in commitment to God, He gives us the desires of our heart because those desires come from Him.

When God created Adam, He placed within Adam the desire for a companion and marriage partner. *However* God didn't immediately create Eve. The Bible teaches that God formed out of the ground all the beasts of the field and all the birds of the air. But for Adam no suitable helper was found. (Gen. 2:19a, 20a)

Adam was a single man with a God given desire for a mate. He wanted someone who would share this beautiful paradise with him. Personally, I don't believe Adam ever begged God for a wife. I don't believe he pouted because he didn't get what he wanted when he wanted it. I certainly don't think he hung out at Eden's Singles Club on Saturday nights. So what did he do?

He went to sleep- but this was not just any sleep. He slept in God's will. Maybe, just maybe, right before he drifted off to sleep, he prayed, that his aching and lonely heart would find solace. Maybe he prayed that his loneliness would be gone when he awoke.

Think with me for a moment. How do you think Adam felt as he watched the animals created by God walk off with their partners and yet here he was alone. Can you identify with him in some area of your life?

What desire is in your heart that you are waiting for God to fulfill and bring to pass?

My friend, it is all about timing- not yours and not mine- but His.

It is all about His way- not yours and not mine.

The Lord caused the man to fall into a deep sleep; while he was sleeping, he took one of the man's ribs and closed up the place with flesh. Then the Lord God made a woman from the rib He had taken out of the man, and He brought her to the man. (Gen. 2:21-22)

In His wisdom, God knew exactly how to meet Adam's desires and in His wisdom He knew when to meet those desires.

God is well aware of those desires in your heart today and He knows how to meet them and when. Commit your way to the Lord and trust Him.

Father, help me to trust You with my dreams and with my future. I want to accomplish every task You have appointed for me, but I will need You to guide me and to lead me. Help me to trust You for the how and when. In Jesus' name.

Day Twelve

Blessing and honor and glory and power Be to Him who sits on the throne, And to the Lamb forever and ever.

Revelation.5:13 NKJV

What a picture the Apostle John gives us of the celebration that awaits us and that we will one day enjoy. John describes four living creatures that surround the throne on which Jesus reigns supreme over the universe. These living creatures never stop saying: "Holy, holy, holy is the Lord God Almighty, who was, and is, and is to come." (Rev. 4:8)

Whenever the living creatures give glory, honor, and thanks to Him who sits on the throne, the twenty-four elders fall down before Him and worship Him. I can only imagine the harmony that rings throughout heaven as worship and praise flow freely from the angelic beings. They cannot contain themselves and so they loudly sing, "Worthy is the Lamb, who was slain to receive power and wealth and wisdom and strength and honor and glory and praise!"

John continues by describing the whole universe, every creature in heaven and on earth and under the earth and on the sea, proclaiming in continuous acclamation: "To Him who sits on the throne and to the Lamb be praise and honor and glory and power forever and ever!"

When you worship Him, you are never worshipping alone. There are angels and the twenty-four elders who never stop their praise and acclamation and worship.

Have you ever felt overwhelmed by a situation in your life? What did you do? Did you worry and struggle? Or did you begin to praise? Praise will NOT solve the situation but it will definitely change you! Praise has the ability to take our eyes off of self and to magnify the One who is worthy. Praise elevates us from the depths of despair to a place of victory!

You don't have to wait until you get to Heaven to join the angels in continuous worship- you can start today.

Praise is contagious! Let me say it again, Praise is contagious!

Who is praising God today because you are?

Father, transform me into a radical worshipper. I want to worship You because of who You are and not just because of what You do. I choose to worship with reckless abandonment. I choose to worship freely and without reservation. I will worship with all my strength and might. In Jesus' name.

Day Thirteen

Therefore, take up the full armor of God that you may be able to resist in the evil day, and having done everything, to stand firm. Stand firm therefore, HAVING GIRDED YOUR LOINS WITH TRUTH, and HAVING PUT ON THE BREASTPLATE OF RIGHTEOUSNESS, and having shod YOUR FEET WITH THE PREPARATION OF THE GOSPEL OF PEACE; in addition to all, taking up the shield of faith with which you will be able to extinguish all the flaming missiles of the evil one. And take THE HELMET OF SALVATION, and the sword of the Spirit, which is the Word of God. With all prayer and petition pray at all times in the spirit…

Ephesians. 6:14-18 NASB

We are instructed to "PUT ON" the full armor of God that we may be able to resist in the evil day. If a soldier were to go to war in a swimsuit, he would become very vulnerable to the enemy. Likewise, when we fail to put on the armor, we become vulnerable to the enemy.

Do you prepare yourself daily to meet the spiritual challenges which will come your way? Do you put your armor on daily?

Let me encourage you to start the day this way:

Lord, I recognize that I am stepping onto a battlefield, but I will not fear for You have given me everything I need to stand firm. In the power of the Holy Spirit, I put on the armor of God.

I thank you for the belt of truth that is wrapped around my waist. I thank you that I walk in the truth of Your Word and I will not be deceived nor misled.

I thank you for my breastplate of righteousness- my heart and emotions will be safe. I refuse to be governed by my feelings which can mislead me. I purpose in my heart to be controlled by the Holy Spirit and not by the flesh.

I thank You for my shoes of peace. I confess that I will walk in peace. Everywhere I go peace is with me. Today, I will stand my ground and I know that You will empower me to stand firm against the philosophies of the world and the attacks of the enemy.

I thank You for my shield of faith. I am not walking by what I see but I am determined to walk by faith. Whenever the enemy hurls his missiles I will not be shaken for I hold up my shield and I am not overcome by his attacks.

I thank You for my helmet of salvation- today I confess that I have the mind of Christ. Therefore, I will have a sharp and attentive mind. I will have creative thoughts and Christ centered thoughts. I will not let my imagination wander to places that could lead to sin. I will guard what my eyes see and what my ears hear.

I thank You for my sword- Your word is a lamp unto my feet and a light unto my path. Today, I will read Your Word and I will have understanding and revelation. I will hide Your Word in my heart that I may not sin against You. Today, I will be transformed by the power of Your Word and by the working of the Holy Spirit.

Help me to pray sincerely and fervently, that I might make a difference in my family, church, community, and country.

Father, I know that I will be attacked by the enemy but I also know that You have equipped me to overcome. Help me to stand firm in You and in the truth of Your word. I will not be intimidated by the enemy's lies- Your Word is my life and banner of truth. In Jesus' Name.

Day Fourteen

The wicked man flees though no one pursues, but the righteous are as bold as a lion.

Proverbs 28:11 NIV

To be a Christian means that we are like Christ. In today's culture, being a Christian can mean that you wear a cross or you go to church, or you are kind and good. The meaning of Christianity has been changed by the world, but not by God.

Jesus was full of God's power, passion, and fire. How did Jesus have this boldness? His boldness was motivated by His love for the Father and the Father's children. This boldness not only motivated Him in love but it drove Him to live a life of obedience.

As a follower of Christ, am I motivated to love like Christ? Am I driven to live a life of obedience?

One of the ways we obey God and show to be Christ-like is when we step into the place of intercession and boldly claim the promises of God for our brothers and sisters who need His power working in their lives.

We need to step into this role and begin to take back that which the enemy has stolen from our lives, our families and from our communities.

Day Fifteen

Truly my soul silently waits for God; From Him comes my salvation. He only is my rock and my salvation. He is my defense; I shall not be greatly moved.

Psalm 62: 1-2 NKJV

Do you like waiting? I *strongly* dislike waiting and very honestly, I don't know many who do. For most of us, waiting can be pure agony. You arrive to your doctor's appointment on time, only to have to wait and wait and wait. You stop by the grocery store to get those few items and get stuck in a long checkout line. Then (this is my favorite) there's the snail paced line at the bank drive-thru. Is it any wonder that it seems like no one in our society likes to wait?

Many times when we take something to the Lord in prayer, we have the tendency to take our human impatience with us. We request something from God and we want an immediate answer. Unfortunately, there are some people that feel that if God doesn't answer their prayer immediately- then He must no longer answer prayer, or at least *not* theirs. He must not be listening or He didn't hear them. That my friends, is a deception of the enemy and if we fall for the lie, it is a great tragedy.

Let's compare that attitude to King David's. David was 16 years of age when God sent the prophet Samuel to anoint him as King. But 16 years would pass before the promise was fulfilled. What did David do during that time? Did he moan and groan and feel forgotten by God? Did he look towards heaven, shake his fist and demand the throne? No, David understood that God could be trusted. David also understood that his heavenly Father was not only the God of *who* and *what* but also of *when* and *how*. David wanted the Kingship not in his own timing but in God's timing. David waited.

What are you waiting on today? Are you waiting impatiently, or like King David, trusting in God's timing and provision?

Day Sixteen

You, my brothers, were called to be free. But do not use your freedom to indulge the sinful nature; rather, serve on another in love.

Galatians 5:13 NIV

There are many people who have the misconception that being "called" by God is something only missionaries, pastors, and other church leaders experience. But the Bible says that everyone is called to serve God by serving others. What a privilege!

We are not saved by serving but we are saved for serving.

Paul gives us three insights in this verse:

First: the basis for serving others is salvation. Paul writes; "you were called to be free." The bottom line is that you and I cannot serve God until Jesus has set us free. Until we are changed by His transforming power, our purpose for serving can be from a wrong or selfish motive.

Second: the barrier to serving others is selfishness. Paul warns, "do not use your freedom to indulge the sinful nature." Let's not become so preoccupied with our own dreams, desires, and agendas that we find ourselves out of time and energy to help others.

Third: the motive for serving is love. Paul writes, "serve one another in love." This is a big key to building family, church, and community. Without love we will find ourselves bankrupt.

Did you know that God is more interested in *why* you serve others than in *how* well you serve them? God is always looking at the heart.

Let me encourage you to serve willingly and eagerly out of love for Jesus and gratitude for all He has done for you.

Father, I recognize that I am more like Jesus when I am washing feet, when I am serving like He did. Help me to become more eager and willing to serve those who are less fortunate and to show your love to others. I want to be mindful that Jesus came to serve and He gave his life on the cross at Calvary so that I could have eternal life. He paid the ultimate price. Help me to be selfless and generous and to serve with a willing and happy heart. In Jesus' Name.

Day Seventeen

Invest what you have, because after a while
you will get a return.

Ecclesiastes. 11:1 NCV

Generosity is its own reward. I can think of no downside to being generous. Don't you find that when you give you get a "natural high" and you desire to give more.

But let's suppose for a moment, that this isn't true- do you think there is a practical benefit or bonus associated with generosity? In Ecclesiastes 11:1, we read, "cast your bread on the surface of the waters, for you will find it after many days." NASB

Truthfully, <u>generosity is an investment</u>. When you are generous with your resources, talents, or time- you will reap the harvest from your acts of generosity. You may be investing in church, people, charities, or causes. However you may not see the return immediately, but God's Word promises that the return will come.

"Be generous; Invest in acts of charity. Charity yields high returns." Eccl. 11:1 The Message

One of my favorite movies is "It's a Wonderful life." George Bailey, the main character of the movie proves that generosity in deed works. He reaps a harvest from his generous giving. In his time of need, the entire town turns out to help him because he had always been there for the town.

As you are given opportunities to practice generous giving, do it and see what God will do for you.

You can give without loving, but you cannot love without giving.

Day Eighteen

I am the Lord your God, who brought you up out of Egypt.
Open wide your mouth and I will fill it.

Psalm 81:10 NIV

Throughout God's Word, we find that our heavenly Father delights in meeting the needs of His children and in fulfilling their desires. However, today there are many Christians walking through life with less than God's best. If God wants to meet our needs (and he does) then how can we come to the place where we avoid missing his blessings?

Psalm 81 gives some insight to this question. The writer tells us of a time when the Israelites missed out on God's best for them. If you have read the book of Exodus, then you know that the Israelites praised God, when He delivered them from bondage. However, it did not take them long to forget what God had done for them and they began to worship other gods.

They complained and grumbled and wanted to go back to Egypt. They developed a very unhealthy pattern of life. They strayed and disobeyed, called on God, received mercy and forgiveness, and then forgot God. Over and over, we see this cycle in the Old Testament. The story of the Israelites reads like a roller coaster ride.

But before we get too critical, let's examine our own lives and the history of our nation.

Verses 8-10 give us God's perspective, "Hear, O my people and I will warn you- if you would but listen to me. O Israel! You shall have no foreign god among you... I am the Lord who brought you up out of Egypt. Open wide your mouth and I will fill it."

Is it possible that some of our unmet needs and desires are a result of disobedience? You and I may not have golden statues in our home that we bow down to and worship. No, our statues are usually less obvious- relationships, careers, finances, hobbies, children, and even ministry. Anything that we put ahead of the Lord becomes an idol.

Will you ask the Lord, today, if there is anything that is hindering you from receiving his blessings? Pay close attention to his answer and then let him help you in that area.

Remember He is always ready to guide you and to bless you. He wants you to be blessed so that you can be a conduit of His blessings to others.

What I worship determines what I become. Anonymous

Day Nineteen

For the eyes of the Lord go to and fro throughout the earth that
He may strongly support those whose heart is completely His.

2 Chronicles 16:9 NASB

Have you ever asked the question, "Can God really use me?" I think
that we have all at some time asked that question. God has the incredible ability of taking ordinary people and using them to do extraordinary things for His Kingdom.

Do you remember a shepherd boy named David? He went from shep-
herding flocks of sheep to becoming the greatest King of Israel.

Gideon went from being a frightened man to a man of valor and courage.

Esther, a simple Jewish girl, saved her people from destruction because
she stood up for what was right.

Deborah was used by God to lead the armies of Israel into battle when
others were afraid.

In the New Testament, Jesus took two ordinary fishermen, Peter and
John, and they went from fishing for fish to fishing for men with boldness and power.

The truth is that God looks for ordinary men and women- like you and me. He is looking for those whose hearts are completely His. Are you an ordinary person? I have great news for you- God is looking for you to turn your part of the world right side up.

God has a definite purpose and calling for every individual. He has a work for you to do. He will strongly support those who truly belong to Him.

God has changed you and me and he wants to use that to bring change in others.

Get ready to be used by the Master!

Father, I am so excited that I qualify to work for You and with You. I qualify not because of my talents or abilities but because I am an ordinary person who serves an extraordinary God. I thank You that You choose to use me, in spite, of my flaws and failings. Thank You Lord for trusting me and letting me work in Your world. In Jesus' name.

Day Twenty

I cry to you for help when my heart is overwhelmed. Lead
me to the towering rock of safety.

Psalm 61:2 NLT

God promises that He will give us a peace that surpasses understanding
but he never promised that this peace would necessarily give us an
understanding of the *why* and *how long*.

I know many who are in the middle of a personal crisis right now.
Perhaps that's you. Maybe today, you are facing a devastating loss
of finances because of the loss of employment, or foreclosure on your
home seems near and real. Maybe your marriage is falling apart and
divorce seems imminent; or possibly you are facing a life-threatening
illness; or maybe it is a prodigal son or daughter that keeps you awake
at night.

If this doesn't describe you- PRAISE GOD! But we all know someone
that is going through these difficulties.

Today, many are finding (believers included) themselves gripped with
fear about the future and its uncertainty.

So what should we do? The Bible has the answer "Be anxious for nothing, but in everything by prayer and supplication with thanksgiving let

your requests be made known to God. And the peace of God, which surpasses all comprehension, shall guard your hearts and your minds in Christ Jesus." Phil. 4:4-6

Regardless of whether we are going through a crisis at this moment or not, we have known times of struggles and the overwhelming feeling of hopelessness.

We have also known the incredible peace that comes from prayer. His peace has overwhelmed us. *Even* in the midst of the storm we have felt His hands comforting us and heard His voice encourage us on.

I am reminded of a song from many years ago, "Give Them All to Jesus" one particular part of the song is: He never said you'd only see sunshine, He never said there'd be no rain. He only promised a heart full of singing about the very things that once brought pain.

Do you need His strength today? Call unto Him and ask for it. He will hear you and He will answer you.

You can talk to God because God listens. Your voice matters in heaven. He takes you very seriously. When you enter His presence, the attendants turn to you to hear your voice. No need to fear that you will be ignored. Even if you stammer or stumble, even if what you have to say impresses no one, it impresses God and He listens. Max Lucado

Day Twenty-One

And as they went to tell his disciples, behold, Jesus met them, saying, "Rejoice!"

Matthew 28:9 NKJV

Jesus' resurrection is an incredible reminder that God gives second chances. When Jesus was crucified, it came as a shock to His follower, that wasn't *their* plan. They didn't seem to understand that He *had* to be crucified and buried. They didn't understand that there would be a resurrection. And when that actually happened, **their faith was shattered and they scattered.**

But after the resurrection, we see the risen Lord seeking those discouraged men who had scattered. For what purpose? Jesus sought them so He could revive them and re-ignite their hearts for His purpose. Jesus could have written them off- He could have reminded them of their failure to stay with Him and to stand by Him. Instead, He chose to restore them.

Mary Magdalen went to Jesus' tomb early in the morning. The angel told her, "He has risen." As Mary Magdalen and the other Mary were en route to tell the other disciples, Jesus met them saying, "Rejoice!" Jesus restored her hope and purpose in life.

Thomas missed the most important meeting of his life, I don't know where he was, but he wasn't in the room when Jesus appeared to the other disciples. As they recounted the story to him- he said, "Unless I see…" Thomas was skeptical but Jesus put his skepticism to rest. He reappeared and said to Thomas, "Reach your finger here, and look at My hands; and reach your hand here, and put it into My side. **Do not be unbelieving, but believing.**" (John 20:27) Thomas the skeptic was restored and he became Thomas the believer.

Do you remember the two discouraged disciples travelling on the road to Emmaus? Jesus spoke to them but they did not recognize him at first. But when he took bread, blessed and broke it, and gave it to them; their eyes were opened and they knew Him. And they said to one another, "**Did not our heart burn within us** while He talked with us on the road, and while He opened the Scriptures to us?" (Luke 24:31-32)

Jesus went out of His way to restore their hope.

Do you have doubts or fears today? The same Jesus who restored Mary Magdalen, the two disciples on the road, and Thomas, the skeptic can and will restore your faith.

Remember, God is the God of second chances and restoration! Doesn't this give you a renewed hope? It sure does to me!

Father, I am overtaken by the depth of Your love, a love that is perfect and unconditional. A love that gave me Your very best- Your son, Jesus Christ. Thank You for the cross, may I always be mindful that the gift of salvation that was free to me was not without cost to the Savior. He shed His blood and His body was broken for me. I thank You for the forgiving me of my sins and for picking me up when I fall. Thank You for second chances and for restoration. Thank You that dead dreams and hopes become alive in You. In Jesus' Name.

Day Twenty~Two

For Zion's sake I will not keep silent. And for Jerusalem's sake
I will not keep quiet, until her righteousness goes forth like
brightness, And her salvation like a torch that is burning.

Isaiah 62:1 NASB

On May 14, 1948, Israel was recognized as a nation by the world. But
in God's eyes, Israel has always had His recognition.

Beginning in Genesis 12 and throughout the Old Testament, it is
God's love story regarding the Jewish people and the nation of Israel,
the apple of His eye. God refers to Israel as He does to no other land
on the earth.

This small piece of land does not go unnoticed by the world. It is interesting that this small area of the world makes the news almost nightly.

History records many of the atrocities that have been committed against
the Jewish people and the attacks on Israel. Many of its enemies would
love to see Israel wiped off the face of the earth. But God has incredible
plans for this nation. No enemy will be able to destroy this land or its
people!

Evangelical Christians have generally supported Israel, Genesis 12:3,
states "God will bless those who bless Israel and will curse the one who

curses Israel." America, as a nation has enjoyed many blessings because of its friendship and alliance with Israel. Let us pray that America will always be a friend to Israel and will stand by her side and be a blessing to her.

Let me share two reasons why we who are followers of the Lord must stand with Israel:

1. **Israel belongs to God.** He created it and can give that land to whom he chooses and he chose to give it to Israel. The title deed belongs to them. Modern day Palestinians have no Biblical mandate to own Israel.

2. **Christians owe a debt of eternal gratitude** to the Jewish people for their contributions, which gave birth to the Christian faith. As Gentiles, we have received the unsearchable riches of the Gospel of Jesus Christ. We enjoy the riches of His love, peace, joy, and countless other blessings. We enjoy the Abrahamic covenant. We are truly blessed.

May I encourage you to pray for the peace of Jerusalem and for the people of Israel?

Day Twenty-Three

...For John baptized with water, but you shall be baptized
with the Holy Spirit not many days from now.

Acts 1:5 NASB

Can you imagine the thoughts that must have been going through the
apostle's minds? They were to wait for what the Father had promised.
The infilling of the Holy Spirit is an incredible blessing. I will never
forget the day that I was born again (invited Jesus to be Lord and Savior) and filled with the Holy Spirit. I will also never forget when the
Holy Spirit began to teach me to move beyond the infilling *into* the
power of the Holy Spirit.

In Luke 4:1, we read that Jesus, full of the Holy Spirit, went into the
wilderness

But notice verse 14, Jesus returned to Galilee in the power of the Holy
Spirit.

In the days, in which we are living, it is not enough to have the infilling
of the Holy Spirit- we must have the power of the Holy Spirit.

There must be a progression of change in our lives that reflects that we
are Spirit empowered men and women.

Perhaps we become frustrated in our calling and giftings because we have not yet learned how to walk in His power.

How do we get there? Is it possible to walk in His power and feel victorious even in the midst of the storm?

I believe it is and I will share three things that will help us walk in Spirit empowered victory:

1. Prayer- in the discipline of our prayer lives we will become more aware and sensitive to the Holy Spirit.

2. Fasting- fasting is one of the most powerful weapons and one of the least used. Fasting is one of the most valuable keys to living a Spirit empowered life. Fasting is giving up food for a specific period and for specific prayer. Fasting will get you the victory over habits, sin, or any other hindrances in your life. Fasting says to God "I am serious."

3. God's Word- we must learn how to skillfully use his Word as a weapon. I encourage you to memorize His word, meditate on His word, and study His Word. Hide His Word in your heart and apply His Word to your daily living.

In these last days, it will not be enough to have church as usual. The church will have to be full of Spirit empowered men and women doing the work of His Kingdom.

"To pray is to open our hearts to Jesus. And Jesus is all that we sinners need, both for time and eternity."

O. Hallesby

Day Twenty-Four

In the same way, you should see yourselves as being dead to
the power of sin and alive with God through Christ Jesus.
So, do not let sin control your life here on earth so that you
do what your sinful self wants to do.

Romans 6:11-12 NCV

Choosing to become a follower of Jesus Christ is a life change- a continual life change. It would be wonderful, if on the day that we asked
Jesus to be Savior and Lord, self would no longer want to sin. Personally, I have not found that to be the case. To the contrary, the more I
try to do what is right, the more intense the battle.

I like what Charles Finney said, "Aim at being perfect. Every young
convert should be taught that if it is not his purpose to live without
sin, he has not yet begun to be a Christian. What is Christianity, but
supreme love to God and a supreme purpose of heart or disposition to
obey God? If there is not this, there is no Christianity at all. It should
be our *constant* purpose (aim) to live wholly to God and obey all His
commandments. We should live so that if we were to sin, it would be
an inconsistency, an exception, an individual case, in which we act
contrary to the fixed and general purpose of our lives."

I would say that this is the essence of a true Christian walk. It should not be that I try to see how much I can get away with or how close I can walk to the world without sinning.

Living a holy life is really not as hard as we make it to be. We have the best example- JESUS. He modeled holiness for us and all we need to do is aim at that standard.

Jesus is the target- aim to be like Him. That's my desire to be like Him. I know that I am going to miss the mark from time to time, but that doesn't deter me from aiming to be like Jesus. No one wants us to succeed more in this walk, than He does; therefore, you can be sure that He will help us.

Walk with your heart wholly submitted to Him and you will find you are walking holy before God and man.

Prayer fails when the desire and effort for personal holiness fail.

E.M. Bounds

Day Twenty-Five

I have strength to overcome all things in the One who
strengthens me.

Phil.4:1 Power N.T.

Has there ever been a time in your life when you felt so overwhelmed-
you just didn't think you could go any further? Unless you are a child,
the answer is yes.

I remember reading an article once and the question asked was, "what
does Jesus expect of you?" I quickly began mentally making a list: obedience, faithfulness, love, compassion, service, etc. But according to
the author of the article, my answers were wrong. The correct answer
was *failure*. I have to be honest with you, that answer really excited me.
At that moment, I didn't care if the author was right, because I knew
that failure was something I could do without even trying. The author
didn't stop there, he said, "God has given you the Holy Spirit so that
you *NEVER* have to fail."

That's right, "without Christ, we can do nothing. But in Christ, we can
do all things."

His strength will hold you up when you can't stand any longer.

His strength will carry you through the desert of life and bring you to an oasis of hope.

His strength will encourage you when you feel despondent and sad.

His strength will carry you when fear paralyzes you and your faith is shattered.

He will strengthen you when you have no more to give.

Our strength will never be sufficient- we must be anchored to Him and depend upon His strength- His strength is perfect!

He did not say we could do some things, or most things; He said I can do all things through Him who strengthens me.

When you grow weary (and you will), be quick to run into His arms and let Him sustain you through any and all things.

Only he who can say, 'The Lord is the strength of my life' can say, 'of whom shall I be afraid?'

Alexander MacLaren

Day Twenty-Six

Woe to them! For they have gone in the way of Cain, have run greedily in the error of Balaam for profit and perished in the rebellion of Korah.

Jude 1:11 NKJV

Balaam was a prophet in the Old Testament and the Bible records that he was greedy for gold. He had been hired by the Moabites to put a curse on Israel. Simply put, he seemed to be a prophet who was willing to work for profit. The Bible tells us that as Balaam was preparing to go and carry out his assignment, God spoke to him and said, "You shall not go with them; you shall not curse the people, for they are blessed." Numbers 22:12

Balaam ultimately ignored God's command. When you read the story, you find that as Balaam was on his way to disobeying God, his donkey saw the angel of the Lord standing in the road with his drawn sword in his hand and the donkey turned off from the way. Balaam began to beat the donkey. It isn't long before God opens the donkey's mouth and the donkey speaks. Notice two questions asked by the donkey: "Am I not your donkey on which you have ridden ever since I became yours, to this day? Was I ever disposed to do this to you?" The donkey had more sense than his master. The Lord opened Balaam's spiritual eyes and he saw the angel of the Lord. The angel's words, "It's a good thing your donkey saved your skin because I was ready to kill you." (my paraphrase)

Why did Balaam disobey God? Because greed overtook him. His greed kept him out of harmony with God's love and God's will.

The dictionary defines greed: *as a selfish and excessive desire for more of something (as money) than is needed.*

Greed will cause us to fail to accomplish the Lord's plans. In the same manner, that greed infected Balaam and kept him out of harmony with God's love and will- it will do the same to you and me.

Selfishness will never help us to succeed in God's Kingdom. We can become so focused on material things and personal success that they become more important than people or anything else.

Generosity, on the other hand, brings God's blessings. Generosity is more than writing a check, it is investing in the lives of others. How can we do this? By serving God's people; visiting the orphans and widows, visiting those who are shut-ins, bringing them encouragement and companionship. Writing a check is easy but investing of self, that's priceless!

Don't let greed keep you out of harmony with the love of God, *but* let generosity flow freely from your heart.

Remember, God loves a cheerful giver!

Life isn't about having, it's about being. Jewish saying

Day Twenty-Seven

To these four young men God gave knowledge and understanding of all kinds of literature and learning. And Daniel
could understand visions and dreams of all kind.

Daniel 1:17 NIV

It is not unusual for companies to spend millions of dollars to influence the public. It isn't just money that is spent but the hours that go into strategizing and planning the best campaign to influence the buyer. Hours are spent as decisions are made to capture the imagination of the general public.

Did you know that you too have influence and capture the attention of others? But there is a huge difference. A company tries to convince you to buy that new car, or that expensive pair of jeans, or the latest gadget. However, your life captures the hearts of people with the Gospel through your godly influence. So you see, you are in a much more important business than large corporations. For you and me to have a positive impact on others, we must and need to present a consistent witness before all men.

We must have a strong conviction about God's Word, because this is the foundation of our faith. We must believe that the Bible is the true and practice living it out daily. Daniel certainly did. When you read the account in chapter one, you find Daniel and his friends refusing the King's food and wine. Why? Daniel understood that the Bible forbid him to eat anything offered to idols. (Exod. 34:15)

Daniel's refusal to eat the food placed before him, put him and his friends in danger of death. BUT Daniel knew that God wanted his obedience. God wants your obedience and mine, no matter what!

For you and me, following the Bible's instructions isn't usually a matter of life and death, but it can sometimes place us in uncomfortable situations. However, what we must remember is that if we are going to have a godly influence in our world, we must be committed to our convictions. Your life may be the only reflection of Jesus seen by others. Like Daniel, we must decide to follow the Lord regardless of the cost. We must stand true to our convictions and watch God use our example to bring others into His Kingdom.

"Let your light shine brightly before all men and God that they might see your good works and glorify God."

A holy life does not live in the closet, but it cannot live without the closet.

E.M. Bounds

Day Twenty-Eight

...from the same mouth come both blessing and cursing.

James 3:10

Words have such power. Our words have the power to encourage, to strengthen, and to build up. Our words also have the power to discourage, to intimidate, and to tear down. What choice have you made? Are you an encourager or a discourager? Are you positive or negative?

Words not only make an impact on others but also on *ourselves.*

What declarations are you making, what are you speaking about yourself and your situation? Are you building yourself up and agreeing with what God's Word says *or* are you confessing the situation in your life, which is only temporary?

Are you struggling with sickness or disease? "By His stripes you are healed." Isaiah 53:5

Are you struggling financially? "My God shall provide all my needs according to His riches in glory in Christ Jesus." Philippians 4:19

Are you struggling emotionally? "He will give you the mantle of praise instead of a spirit of fainting." Isaiah 61:3

Are you struggling with anxiety? "Cast all your cares on Him because He cares for you." 1 Peter 5:7

Are you fearful about tomorrow? "Therefore, do not be anxious for tomorrow, for tomorrow will care for itself." Matthew 6:34; "Jesus Christ is the same yesterday, today, and forever." Hebrews 13:8; "He will never abandon you nor forsake you." Hebrews 13:5b

Declare with your mouth what God says and you will discover that although your circumstances may remain the same (for a season) - you will be changed inwardly.

Words have power! What kind of power do they have in your life?

Words must be weighed not counted. Anonymous

Day Twenty-Nine

In the beginning was the Word, and the Word was with
God, and the Word was God. He was God in the beginning. All things came through Him, and there was not one
thing that came into being without His participation.

John 1:1-3 Power N.T

Over two thousand years ago, God chose to do the unimaginable- He
chose to send His son to earth, to live among us and to be our bridge
back to God. Man had lost his way and there was only One who could
bring us back- Jesus the Messiah. I can only imagine the activity in
heaven, as God sent His only Son to earth, to put on human flesh and
to walk the journey of humanity. For 33 years Jesus lived among us and
in those short years, He accomplished the perfect will of the Father.

Jesus was destined for the cross so that you and I could have an eternal
destiny. Our salvation came at the expense of His life: He was mocked,
spat upon, rejected by man, beaten until He was barely recognizable,
crowned with thorns (not placed) but pressed into his skull, and finally
nailed to a cross on Calvary. His blood was shed for you and me.

Never forget what price was paid for your salvation.

Never forget His great love for you.

Never forget that you have an eternal hope because of His obedience.

Never forget your name has been written in the Lamb's book of Life with His blood.

Never forget that He's coming back for you!

Day Thirty

But let patience have her perfect work, that ye may be perfect and entire, wanting nothing.

James 1:4 KJV

The word "perfect" means mature. So the trying of your faith works patience that you may be mature, entire, wanting or lacking for nothing. Isn't this where you want to be? Don't you want to be that person- mature, entire, and wanting or lacking for nothing? How do we get there?

We have to learn about patience- Bible patience. The word patience in verse 4 means "to be steadfast." Another definition is to remain constant. Notice what it says, "the trying of your faith worketh patience." Faith and patience are linked together. It is your faith that is being tried and patience is developing from it.

Throughout the New Testament, there are several references where faith and patience are mentioned together. For the sake of brevity, I will mention only one. (This would make an excellent study)

Hebrews 12:1: tells us that we are to "run the race with patience, looking unto the author and finisher of our faith, Jesus."

I believe that Scripture clearly teaches that for us to receive the promises of God- faith, patience, and love are required.

With that said, then, I must make a decision to choose what God wants for my life.

I choose then to follow after righteousness. I am in right standing with God because of what Jesus did at Calvary and because I have chosen to follow Him and His ways.

I choose to follow after godliness. I will have a God-like attitude in my words, thoughts, and deeds.

I choose to follow after faith. I walk by faith and not by sight. "Without faith it is impossible to please God, for he who comes to God must believe that He is and that He is a rewarder of those who seek Him." (Hebrew 11:6)

I choose to follow after love. God is love. I am most like Him when I am walking in love.

I choose to follow after patience. I will wait on the Lord and trust Him to complete the process of maturing in my life.

I choose to fight the good fight of faith. It's a good fight because I have already won in Jesus.

I will apply God's word to my heart and life and I will welcome faith, patience, and love to develop in me. I will be a man/woman of God who lacks or wants for nothing.

One of the greatest disadvantages of hurry is that it takes such a long time.

G.K. Chesterton

Day Thirty-One

Both riches and honor come from You, and You reign over all. In Your hand is power and might; in Your hand is to make great and to give strength to all.

1Chron. 29:12 NKJV

God's crowning jewel of creation was man. Man was created with a distinct purpose and for a divine purpose. When we live this purpose out- life is rewarding and fulfilling.

However, if God's purpose is rejected or ignored, life will never be what it was meant to be. Look around and you will see many who have rejected the purpose of God for their lives; consequently, their lives are not what God intended.

But you will also find many who have chosen to know and fulfill the purpose of God for their life. The result is that they are fulfilled and life has meaning.

A light bulb is just a simple glass globe. When it is in the box it is useless and has no significant meaning. However, take that same bulb out of its box and fit it into a lamp and plug it into a power source, and suddenly that useless bulb brightens the room and fulfills its purpose for existence. That light bulb was created to give light and because it is fulfilling its purpose we don't have to walk around in the dark.

When we try and separate ourselves from the Father's purpose, we are like that bulb in the box- created with purpose but lying in a meaningless existence. But when we plug into the power source through our relationship with Jesus, then and only then, will our lives be what they were created to be. God's purposes for you were created uniquely for you. God's purposes for my life were created uniquely for me.

As we walk intimately with Him- we will be able to discern His will and purpose for our lives. He wants to reveal His purpose to us at every crossroad of life.

Day Thirty-Two

All Scripture is God inspired and useful for teaching, for
reproof, restoration, for training in righteousness, so that
the man of God would be able to meet all demands, since
he has been equipped perfectly for every good work.

2 Tim. 3:16-17 Power N.T.

An unprepared soldier will not last against the enemy. Since believers
are at war with Satan, it is necessary that we train and prepare wisely. Training wisely will help our hearts stay pure and our testimony
strong.

How then do I prepare and stay strong?

A soldier must acknowledge the war. The Bible is very clear- you
have an enemy and he has come to steal, kill and destroy. His plans are
destructive towards you. Since you know this, you must recognize that
you are at war.

A soldier must know the enemy. Satan's methods and tricks are
recorded in Scripture for your benefit. He is deceptive, manipulative,
and he is a liar who tries to sabotage your walk with the Lord. Satan
has used deception since the Garden of Eden and he has found that it

continues to work for him today. *Know your enemy as well as he knows you.*

A soldier must undergo training. Everyday believers are given the opportunity to demonstrate their trust in God in at least some small way. These opportunities will serve as preparation for the future when the *big* tests come (and they will come) your way.

A soldier must know how to use his weapons. God's Word is the most effective weapon against the enemy, it is necessary to know His word so that you can have victories. Jesus did not answer the Devil with, "I think," or "I heard," or "I read," Jesus answered- "IT IS WRITTEN." That must be our declaration!

A soldier must resist the lies. Satan will use any worldly means possible to entice you. He will use entertainment and media industries, educational systems, and false religions. These are just a few of his tools. Knowing this, *you* as a believer in Christ, must be wise in deciding what you allow into your mind.

A prepared soldier is one who is Spirit empowered, full of Jesus, and His Word.

A Spirit filled warrior **will not** be exempt from Satan's attacks *but* a Spirit filled warrior **will be** victorious against his attacks through the Blood of Jesus and the authority of Jesus' Name.

The prayer closet is the battlefield of the church, the base of supplies for the Christian and the church. Cut off from it there is nothing left but retreat and disaster.

E.M. Bounds

Day Thirty-Three

And if I go and prepare a place for you, I will come again, and receive you to Myself; that where I am, there you may be also.

John 14:3 NASB

In the book of Genesis, we are told that God was purposefully creating. "And the Lord God planted a garden toward the east, in Eden; and there He placed the man whom He had formed. And out of the ground the Lord God caused to grow every tree that is pleasing to the sight and good for food..." Genesis 2:8-9.

In my imagination, I picture the Father on His hands and knees, digging in the dirt- planting trees and shrubs, flowers and grass. I picture the Father watering and pruning and doing all the work that is necessary in gardening. As He looks over His work, He is pleased and sees the beauty of this perfect and wonderful home. It had to be perfect- it was for His children, Adam and Eve. Imagine with me, the joy that must have been in Father's heart as He handed the keys to Adam; a home that had been lovingly and perfectly prepared for him. Eden wasn't just a home with the basic needs but it was extravagant and beautiful beyond words.

As I think about His preparations for the first earthly home, I become so overwhelmed thinking about the preparations being made for our heavenly home. Do you want a peek at your new home? Read Revelation 21.

In our new home, there will be no more pain, no more crying, no more pain and suffering, no more death. There are no hospitals in heaven, no divorce, no abuse, no financial calamities, no fears, and no heartache.

As wonderful as all these things are, our greatest joy will be that we will be in His presence and never be separated from Him.

We are one day closer to shouting hallelujah around His throne!

"The resurrection of the body…declares that God will make good and bring to perfection the human project He began in the Garden of Eden."

Timothy George

Day Thirty-Four

We are assured *and* know that [God being a partner in their labor] all things work together *and* are [fitting into a plan] for good to *and* for those who love God and are called according to [His] design and purpose.

God has always ruled with supreme authority. There is nothing that is hidden from His knowledge and there is nothing that is beyond the scope of His control.

It is because of His sovereignty, that we who are followers in Christ can rest assured in the assurance of the following:

- God works for your good- The Word teaches that God has the power to work every circumstance in our life into something that is good and beneficial. Remember Joseph? He went from the pit to prison to position. God knew that famine was coming and he sent Joseph ahead to preserve a remnant on the earth. God is doing a work in you to accomplish His will and purpose.

- God's protection is with you everyday- Scripture teaches, "The angel of the Lord encamps around those who fear Him." (Psalm 34:7) Nothing can touch you, the child of God, apart from His permissive will. When you are facing things that are hard and challenging, trust in God's unchanging nature and His enduring promises.

- God has control over your future- He has a plan for you and every member of the family of God. Things which "eye has not seen and ear has not heard, and which have not entered the heart of man, all that God has prepared for those who love Him." (1 Cor. 2:9) You can place your trust in Him because His plans and character are perfect.

Father, I choose today, to trust in You and in Your sovereign ways. I rest in the fact that You are for me and not against me and that the plans You have for me are good and for my best. In Jesus' Name. Amen

Day Thirty-Five

Let them give thanks to the Lord for His lovingkindness,
And for His wonders to the sons of men.

Psalm 107:15 NASB

Every year, we celebrate a holiday known as Thanksgiving Day. It is a day set apart to remember to give thanks for the bounty we have received from a gracious and loving Father.

But should that be the only day, in which we remember to give thanks? The obvious answer is "NO."

We who live in America have been abundantly blessed and have so much to be grateful for; thanksgiving should flow from our heart freely.

Reasons I am thankful:

- I am thankful for my salvation. I did not deserve it nor could I ever earn it-He paid a debt I could not pay!

- I am thankful for His love- before I ever loved Him, He loved me.

- I am thankful to be an American. America is not perfect but it is still the most wonderful nation on the earth.

- I am thankful for His grace and mercy.

- I am thankful for my family, who encourages and supports me.

- I am thankful for my friends, who love and accept me in spite of my faults.

- I am thankful for the freedom to worship.

- I am thankful for what the past has taught me. I am thankful that today, I will walk in His will. I am thankful for an eternal future.

- I am thankful that He picked me to be His child and to be a member in His "forever" family.

What are you thankful for today? Offer Him a bouquet of thanksgiving and gratitude.

Day Thirty-Six

Therefore you must be praying in this way: Our Father, Who
is in the heavens: Your name must at once be made holy:
Your Kingdom must now come: Your will must be done right
now, as in heaven also on earth; You must now give us today
the things necessary for our existence: You must right now
forgive our sins for us, in the same manner as we have com-
pleted forgiving everyone of everything, big and little, against
us: And do not lead us into temptation, but You must now
rescue us from the evil one. For if You would forgive *all other
people* their transgressions, your heavenly Father will also forgive you; but if you would not forgive *all other people,* neither
will your Father forgive your sins.

Mt. 6:9-15 Power N.T.

The Scriptures clearly teach that we are to forgive those who hurt, of-
fend, or mistreat us. Is forgiving easy for you? I must confess that it has
not always been easy for me. There have been times in my life that I
have had to begin by asking the Lord to help me forgive.

Let me share some practical ways that will help us walk in forgiveness:

1. The subject of forgiveness must be taken seriously. It is not something that we should attempt to dismiss casually.

2. You and I must assume full responsibility. Don't blame others for your feelings or actions.

3. Confess it honestly. Be specific with God about your feelings and acknowledge that unforgiveness is sin.

4. Face your anger. Resentment, if it is not dealt with, *can* and *will* open the door to bitterness later on in life.

5. Pray for the other person. I assure you (from personal experience) that this will not be easy in the beginning, but allow the Holy Spirit to help you and you will find freedom.

6. Ask for forgiveness, if the other person is aware that you have been holding resentment or anger towards them.

7. Don't let the enemy imprison you through unforgiveness. Once you have resolved the matter, don't go back and replay the hurt or offense.

Is this process easy? No, but it works. May I suggest that you keep this list handy and that at anytime you feel any thought of resentment or unforgiveness trying to sneak back into your life, immediately go back and repeat the process.

Forgiveness is love in action.

Father, help me forgive and to forgive quickly. I have been forgiven through Your incredible act of love, help me love as You do. I ask in Jesus Name.

Day Thirty-Seven

For this reason we have not stopped praying for you since
the day we heard about you. We ask, God to fill you with the
knowledge of His will through every kind of spiritual wisdom and insight. We ask this so that you will live the kind of
lives that prove you belong to the Lord. Then you will want
to please Him in every way as you grow in producing every
kind of good work by the knowledge about God. We ask
Him to strengthen you by His glorious might with all the
power you need to patiently endure everything with joy. You
will also thank the Father, who has made you able to share
the light, which is what God's people inherit. God has rescued us from the power of darkness and has brought us into
the kingdom of His Son, whom He loves. His Son paid the
price to free us, which means that our sins are forgiven.

Colossians 1:9-14 God's Word Translation

Praying for someone is a great privilege. We know that the power is not
in the praying but in God's response to the prayer. He is moved by our
sincere prayer. The above prayer is a great example for us:

- *Be filled with the knowledge of God's will-* what a great request to offer up on behalf of our family, friends, church, and country. Lord, we want to know your perfect will.

- *Live the kind of lives that prove you belong to God-* I want to walk in a manner worthy of the Lord. Lord, I don't want a temporary change- change me for eternity.

- *Then you will want to please Him-* our goal should be Christ-centered. Lord, may my conversation, conduct, and character please and honor you.

- *As you grow producing every kind of good work-* help me be a producer of what you desire, and let my service unto You glorify you. Lord, help me grow in You and walk in deeper intimacy with You.

- *We ask Him to strengthen you-* in the times in which we are living; we must have God's supernatural power to sustain us. Lord, keep us under the shadow of your wings- that is where we draw strength.

- *You will also thank the Father, who has made you able to share the light-* thank You that You have chosen us to be Your vessels of love and light. Lord, we want our lives to be living epistles of Your power and grace.

Father, thank You for the privilege of prayer and for the ministry of intercession. Thank You for transferring me from a kingdom of darkness into a kingdom of light, and that my life is a testimony of Your mercy and grace. In Jesus' Name.

Day Thirty-Eight

Do not fret or have anxiety about anything, but in every circumstance and in everything by prayer and petition (definite requests) with thanksgiving, continue to make your wants known to God. And God's peace (shall be yours, that tranquil state of a soul assured of its salvation through Christ, and so fearing nothing from God and being content with its earthly lot of whatever sort that is, that peace)which transcends all understanding shall garrison *and* mount guard over your hearts and minds in Christ Jesus.

Philippians 4:6-7 Amplified

Are you in need of some fresh and new blessings in your life?

As you approach the Father asking for these blessings, don't forget to look back at past blessings and to come to Him with a thankful heart.

A thankful heart is pleasing to God and He prefers that we come to him with humility of heart rather than a demanding attitude.

Have you ever been in the grocery store and watched as some little one had a tantrum because his demands were not met immediately? Let's not be guilty of behaving in a childish manner and having an "I want it now" attitude, but let's behave in a childlike manner.

In Luke 17, there is a story told of ten lepers who called out to Jesus for healing, all ten received their healing *but* only one returned to give thanks. He demonstrated a heart of thanksgiving.

I have often asked myself, which category do I fall in? Am I like the nine, who just keep going or am I like the one who returns to thank Jesus? What about you?

I believe the heart of God is grieved when we are thankless and when our attitude reflects ingratitude.

Will you thank Him today?

Father, "I will enter Your gates with thanksgiving in my heart and I will enter Your courts with praise." How can I offer anything less than thanksgiving to You? You have blessed me beyond what I deserve. I purpose in my heart to thank You and to acknowledge Your blessings over my life. I will testify of the goodness and mercy of my God. In the precious name of Jesus.

Day Thirty-Nine

And your ears will hear a word behind you, "this is the way, walk in it," whenever you turn to the right or to the left.

Isaiah 30:21 NASB

The Father in His goodness has given us very clear directions on how to live a blessed life. He has given us His Word and His Holy Spirit to guide us into victory and success every day.

There are three keys to living this life:

1. To do justly: this means that we are to be honest, honorable, and conscientious towards God, our fellow man, and ourselves.

2. Love mercy: Let's define mercy- it is undeserved forgiveness. May I be honest? I love it when God shows mercy to me, but I have not always been quick to show it to others and there have been times I have wanted God to hold back His mercy on others.

3. Walk humbly with God: You and I must devote ourselves to the purpose of knowing God, *not just knowing about* Him. Our desire should be to fall more deeply in love with Him and to know Him more intimately.

We will need to have personal discipline to follow these keys and we will need to remove every form of pride in our lives.

Make it your chief purpose to follow God's ways and then enjoy reaping the rewards for your obedience.

He hath shewed thee, O man, what is good; and what doth the Lord require of thee, but to do justly, and to love mercy, and to walk humbly with thy God?

Micah 6:8

Day Forty

Therefore, my beloved brethren, be steadfast, immovable,
always abounding in the work of the Lord, knowing that
your toil is not in vain in the Lord.

1 Corinthians 15:58 NASB

Have you ever asked yourself, "How effective is the work I do for the
Lord?" After all, I am not a Billy Graham or a Mother Teresa. I am but
one person in the vastness of this great earth- so what am I really ac-
complishing for God.

In the same way that Paul encouraged the Corinthians, the Holy Spirit
encourages you today:

Be steadfast- be faithful in what God has called you to do. That is all
He requires of you. He doesn't expect you to win the whole world, but
are you a living witness to your co-workers and neighbors.

Immovable- stand strong on your foundation in Jesus Christ. Do not
let yourself get trapped by the philosophies of this world. Take a stand
for God's principles and refuse to bow to the god of this world.

Abound in His work- God has allowed us the privilege to work in His vineyard and we are to abound in this work. Your prayers and intercession do not go unnoticed by God.

Day Forty-One

Then one of the evil ones who was hanging there was blaspheming Him saying, "Are You not the Messiah? You must now save Yourself and us." But the other said, rebuking him, "Do you not yourself fear God, because you are in the same sentence? But we indeed justly, for what we did *is* worthy of *what* we are receiving: but this One did nothing improper. Then he was saying, "Jesus, You must right away remember me when You would enter Your Kingdom." Then He said to him, "Truly I say to you, this very day you will be with Me in Paradise."

Luke 23:39-43 Power N.T.

Several years ago, as I was reading these particular verses, there was something that really caught my attention.

First: there is the thief that questioned if Jesus was the Messiah. He was in a predicament that needed a miracle for deliverance. He didn't ask for mercy or forgiveness. He made an unwise decision: he chose to die in his sin.

Second: there was the wise thief; he recognized that he justly deserved his fate and that he was a sinner. But he made a wise decision: he chose to die to sin.

Third: Jesus is on the cross, not for some crime He committed, for He had done nothing wrong. He had fed the thousands, healed the sick, and raised the dead. He had performed miracle after miracle. Jesus went to Calvary because He was the perfect lamb that could be offered on behalf of sinful man. He was the perfect atonement for you and me. Jesus chose to die for sin.

He made the One who did not know sin to be sin on our behalf, so that we ourselves would know the righteousness of God by means of Him. 2 Corinthians 5:2

Today, there are still many, who like the first thief, will choose to die in their sin. They reject Jesus Christ and hold onto their sin. The issue of salvation is not sin- it is whether you and I accept or reject Jesus Christ.

Then there are those like the second thief. You and I are in that category. We made a choice to confess our sins and to ask Jesus to be the Savior and Lord of our lives. We recognized that we needed a Savior and we needed (and still do) His mercy and grace.

If you are reading this devotional and you have never invited Jesus to be your personal Lord, I want to lead you in a prayer:

Father, I admit that I am a sinner and I cannot save myself. Please forgive me of my sins. I repent of all my sins and I invite Jesus to come and reign in my heart as Lord and Savior. I surrender my will and I ask you to help me follow your will. I thank you for welcoming me into your family.

{If this was the first time, you prayed this prayer, or maybe you just made a new commitment; I want to encourage you to find a Bible teaching church, tell someone that you have given your life to Jesus, get into God's Word, and I want to welcome you into the family of God.}

Day Forty-Two

Let us then fearlessly and confidently and boldly draw near to the throne of grace (the throne of God's unmerited favor to us sinners), that we may receive mercy (for our failures) and find grace to help in good time for every need (appropriate help and well-timed help, coming just when we need it).

Hebrews 4:16 Amplified

When was the last time you approached God's throne fearlessly and with confidence and boldness? Approach God fearlessly? YES! Confidently? YES! Boldly? YES!

That's what He wants you to do- God doesn't want you to come to Him in fear and timidity. NO, you're His kid and He wants you to have confidence to come close to your Daddy.

He wants you to bring your fears, worries, cares, and frustrations to Him. He can handle them- He's the God who holds the mountains in one hand and the oceans in the other- those are big hands- and He holds you in those big hands.

Remember the kid's song: He's got the whole world in His hands. That my friend is solid theology!

You don't need an appointment to come to His throne- you can come day or night, morning or night. He's waiting for you.

Be encouraged that your Father is waiting for you and He never grows tired of your visits. He waits and waits for you to approach his throne fearlessly, confidently, and boldly.

What do you need? Tell daddy God!

Day Forty-Three

For who is this uncircumcised Philistine, that he should
taunt the armies of the living God.

1 Samuel 26b NASB

The story of David and Goliath is well known and it teaches modern
day believers about a faith that conquers. In every person's life there
comes a day when you encounter a Goliath. Your "giant" may be human or it may be an overwhelming situation. It may come disguised
as a disease that is taking its toll on your body; it may be the pain of
rejection or the tragedy of loss.

When these "giants" come into our lives, we can cower and faint or we
can do as David and trust God to see us through.

David had experienced God's faithfulness in the past and he knew that
God would remain faithful. I Samuel 17:36, portrays the shepherd boy,
David, telling the story of God giving him victory over a lion and a
bear that threatened the flock entrusted to him.

What about you? Can you look back and see the faithfulness
of God in your life? We all face those faith stretching moments,
but we can also look back and see the memorial stones of His steadfast
faithfulness in our lives.

David spent hours in God's presence and he grew in faith and trust. When you and I spend time with God in prayer and in His Word then like David, we will grow in faith and trust. Trusting the Lord gives you the courage to face those "giants." You and I are able to respond to difficult times on the basis of three important truths:

First: You have your identity in Christ. You have been adopted by the Father and the Holy Spirit dwells in you.

Second: You must know Who Christ is in you: He is your Savior, provider, healer, deliverer, healer, joy giver, peace, burden bearer, redeemer, and your LORD!

Third: In Christ you have the promise of access to Almighty God. (Hebrews 4:16)

A victorious believer is one who knows how to endure and will trust God to make him/her adequate to go through any situation.

You are not facing the "giants" alone. The Holy Spirit dwells in you and He knows that you cannot do this in your strength.

When you trust in God and depend on Him- you will conquer the "Goliath" in your life.

Father, I want to learn to endure in the battles of life. I want to conquer the "giants" that try to defeat me and I want to stand strong in the battle.

Strengthen me Holy Spirit and help me to have an overcoming attitude. I am more than an overcomer and I will not quit until I have the victory. In the mighty name of Jesus. Amen.

Day Forty-Four

But you are A CHOSEN RACE, A royal PRIESTHOOD, A HOLY NATION, A PEOPLE FOR *GOD'S* OWN POSSESSION, that you may proclaim the excellencies of Him who has called you out of darkness into His marvelous light; for you once were not a people, but now you are THE PEOPLE OF GOD; you had not RECEIVED MERCY, but now you have RECEIVED MERCY.

1 Peter 2:9-10 NASB

Has there ever been a time in your life, when you just weren't too sure of God's purpose for your life?

I know that I have struggled with this question, but I have found that the times I struggle the most is when I allow the busyness of day to day life to control me.

In the daily grind of our day- it is easy to forget how wonderfully, fearfully, and purposely designed we are in the eyes of our Creator. The above Scripture brings our focus back to God, and fills us with hope.

We are God's chosen race. There is no need for bickering for a place at the banquet table- He chose you.

The God who placed the moon and stars in place, that tells the sun where to rise, the God who created everything for His good pleasure, He chose you to be a part of His Kingdom.

We are members of a royal priesthood. In Old Testament times, a King could not be a priest and a priest could not be a King; these were two distinct positions.

But in Christ, you are the son or daughter of a King because of the relationship you have with Jesus. You are also a royal priest in the Kingdom of God.

We are a holy nation. The word "holy" means "set apart."

You have been marked as God's child by the Holy Spirit; He placed an eternal seal on your spirit. (Eph. 1:13)

We are God's own possession. Here is one of the most incredible thoughts: Father God sees so much value in you that He purchased your salvation at great cost- the life of His only Son!

There is nothing about your shortcomings, sins, or circumstances that has ever taken Him by surprise.

He is all-knowing, all-powerful, and ever-present.

You are valuable to Him because He created you to be His unique representative on this earth.

You were created on purpose for a divine purpose!

Day Forty-Five

Blessed be the God and Father of our Lord Jesus Christ,
who has blessed us with every spiritual blessing in the
heavenly places in Christ, just as He chose us in Him before
the foundation of the world, that we should be holy and
blameless before Him. In love He predestined us to adop-
tion as sons through Jesus Christ to Himself... In Him we
have redemption through His blood... In Him also we have
obtained an inheritance...

Ephesians 1:3-11 NASB

There are four incredible truths in these verses: (I encourage you to meditate on these verses),

1. Chosen by God: That's right, **you** have been chosen by God. Have you ever been rejected? If you're like me, you have known rejection a time or two, but not from God. Man rejects but God accepts. Go look in the mirror and say I have been chosen by God and I am a person of value because He has given me purpose and worth.

2. Liberated: Once we were shackled by the chains of the flesh and the world. We obeyed the desires of the flesh. We were blind, but then our eyes were opened to the truth. Freedom came and broke the shackles of bondage! Now we are free! The hold the Devil had on us "he ain't got no more!"

3. Redeemed by God: Jesus' death on the cross satisfied Heaven's justice because His perfect life met every Biblical requirement, (Deuteronomy 17:1). He was the perfect Lamb Who willingly shed His blood for your sins and mine. Our sins are forgiven! You and I have a relationship with Him and we are partners with Him in the work of the Kingdom.

"For the wages of sin is death, but the free gift of God is eternal life in Christ Jesus our Lord." (Romans 6:23)

4. Citizens of heaven: we have a living hope through His resurrection from the dead to obtain an inheritance which is imperishable and undefiled and will not fade away, reserved in heaven for you, (1 Peter 1:4).

Don't measure wealth by your bank account or by the things you possess. God measures wealth and success differently than we do.

The truth is that you and I have a spiritual inheritance that is out of this world!

Day Forty-Six

But Moses said to the people, "Do not fear! Stand by and see the salvation of the Lord which He will accomplish for you today...." Then the Lord said to Moses, "Why are you crying out to Me? Tell the sons of Israel to go forward. And as for you, lift up your staff and stretch out your hand over the sea and divide it and the sons of Israel shall go through the midst of the sea on dry land."

Exodus 14:13,15 NASB

Living by faith guarantees hardship. Didn't that sentence just excite you? No one likes to go through hard times, but the truth is that believers who choose to completely surrender to God and obey His laws will experience suffering at times. There is no human being on the face of the earth that is exempt from hardships. Believer in Jesus or not, all will at some time experience hardships.

Moses had to make a choice: sit and have a pity party or *go forward in faith*- in spite of his problems. Moses had left the comfort of the palace to obey the Lord. He knew that he had to go forward.

His life was marked by challenge and sacrifice. But more than that was the fact that his life was shaped by an intimate relationship with God. Every difficulty that came along served to chip away at his self-trust and to strengthen his faith in God. When a new challenge arose, he didn't turn to man or to his culture; he didn't seek the counsel of others- he sought the counsel of God. He turned to God for wisdom and guidance.

1st Peter 4:12 tells us that we are "not to be surprised at the fiery ordeal among you, which comes upon you for your testing, as though some strange thing were happening to you…"

Hardships, difficulties, and suffering are inevitable. Regardless of how hard you try to avoid them, you will not succeed.

Suffering produces character. Suffering takes us to the Lord. There is a level of intimacy that is developed in the midst of the fire. When you look at the life of Moses you see this too be true.

Where are you today? Is everything in your world beautiful and wonderful? Or are you going through such a difficult time that you can't see how you will ever get out of the mess? Are the hardships of life weighing you down?

Make the wise decision- meet the challenge and go forward.

Remember you are not alone- He promised to "never leave you nor forsake you."

Day Forty-Seven

So I urge first for everything to be done in supplications,
prayers, intercessions, thanksgivings on behalf of Kings and
all those who are in authority, so that we would lead a quiet
and tranquil life in reverence and in all godliness.

First Timothy 2:1-2 The Power N.T.

2009 gave America its most historic inauguration. The world watched
as President George Bush stepped down from office and President-elect
Barack Hussein Obama II took office.

America's democracy has been the envy of many. Her transition of
power is exchanged without gunfire or fear of retribution. This democracy is one of the things that makes America so great. She is not perfect
but she is still the land of the free and the home of the brave.

Our founding fathers established this nation on the foundation of
God's Word and His principles. We are a Christian nation. When you
visit Washington D.C., you cannot help but notice the Word of God
inscribed on the walls of marble and granite on the Lincoln Memorial
and the Jefferson Memorial. Have we forgotten that God is not so interested in His name being plastered on walls of stone as much as He
prefers that His name be written on the hearts of flesh?

Every President and his administration face insurmountable problems when they take the reins of the presidency. Whether the office is filled by a Republican or Democrat- the problems are still there.

The problems that face this nation are many: economy, war, poverty, homelessness, healthcare, etc. But the greatest problem that faces our nation is that of moral depravity.

We have become the people, Isaiah warned about in chapter five, "Woe to those who call evil good, and good evil; Who substitute darkness for light and light for darkness; Who substitute bitter for sweet, and sweet for bitter! Woe to those who are wise in their own eyes, and clever in their own sight!"

We who are followers of the Lord Jesus Christ must stand in the gap and pray for this nation and for its leaders. America desperately needs a revival of righteousness and a standard of integrity.

We must pray for the conversion of hearts and for those who are in leadership to have a genuine conversion and call this nation to repentance.

I believe that God still has a purpose and plan for America- will you intercede for her and will you call upon the mercy of God for your beloved country?

Day Forty-Eight

Love one another with brotherly affection as members of one family, giving precedence *and* showing honor to one another. Never lag in zeal and in earnest endeavor; be aglow *and* burning with the Spirit, serving the Lord. Rejoice *and* exult in hope; be steadfast and patient in suffering *and* tribulation; be constant in prayer.

Romans 12:10-12 Amplified Bible

When you read the Gospels, there is something that is very apparent: Jesus loved to talk to His Father. He sought those opportunities to be alone with His Father and to just sit at His feet and fellowship with Him.

There were also times when Jesus spoke to His Father before large crowds, at other times, He asked a few of his disciples to join him. I want you to capture the picture of Jesus longing to be in His Father's presence. He frequently visited with His Father.

Jesus knew the perfect will of the Father because He had been with the Father. Jesus taught us by example how to know God's will- PRAYER.

Jesus took his lead from the Father and did only what the Father said- He understood that He was in partnership with the God of Heaven and Earth. He understood that He was working for the Kingdom of God.

When you and I become serious about prayer, our intimacy with the Lord grows and matures. The more we know Him, the clearer we can recognize His voice. In prayer, our perspective changes from *about us to about Him.* We begin to get a divine perspective and our prayer becomes "not my will but yours."

The more we pray the purer our heart. Prayer should have a purifying effect on us. Our speech and attitudes should reflect the heart of the Father.

The Holy Spirit will guide us in our prayers- He will pray with us and through us.

There are so many benefits to prayer but none as wonderful as the joy of spending time with the Lord.

Seek His presence and not His presents!

Day Forty-Nine

For I know the plans that I have for you, declares the Lord,
plans for welfare and not for calamity to give you a future
and a hope. Then you will call upon Me and come and pray
to Me, and I will listen to you. You will seek Me and find
Me when you search for Me with all your heart.

Jeremiah 29:11-13 NASB

It is not uncommon for us to speculate on what the future holds for us.
Will life be kind or harsh? Rich or poor? Married or single? Children
no children?

Question after question floods our minds. It would be wonderful if
we had a glimpse into the future to see some of the answers to some of
these questions. Or would it?

The reality of life is that we do not know what tomorrow will bring,
but we know the God that holds tomorrow. The uncertainties of the
future will always be there but the assurances of God's Word outweigh
any questions regarding the future.

Read the Scripture carefully:

For I know... He is not confused about your life or mine. He knows
exactly where you are going and how you will get there.

Plans to give you a future and a hope... God is looking to bless you not curse you. He wants what's best for you.

Call upon Me and come and pray to Me and I will listen... When you call upon His name He is already there. He invites you to come and to pray. There is an open invitation for you.

You will seek Me and find Me... the condition for this is that you search for Him with all your heart. Go after God with an undivided heart.

Trust Him with your future- He is more than able to direct you. Trust Him with everything you possess. He is more than able to take care of you. Ask Him to help you trust- He knows you can't do it by yourself.

"Never be afraid to trust an unknown future to a known God." Corrie Ten Boom

Day Fifty

Think constantly of those in prison as if you were prisoners at their side. Think too of all who suffer for you still live in this world.

Hebrews 13:3 J.B. Phillips Translation

In America, we still have the privilege to worship freely, but in many parts of the world that freedom has been lost.

We have brothers and sisters throughout different parts of the world that worship secretly or in underground churches because of the persecution they face. Their opposition is not only from their respective governments but from family and friends. They are our family. They have chosen to follow Christ and they know that it has come with a price.

They have lost homes and possessions; they have been tortured and imprisoned and many have even given their lives for the sake of the Gospel.

We in America, at this time, (I hope we never do) do not suffer persecution, as our brothers and sisters in many parts of the world. Our idea of persecution is being ridiculed or disliked for our faith.

We enjoy the pleasure of sitting in comfortable chairs in our comfortable churches and I don't think any person is in fear that they will be hauled off to jail for coming together in worship. None of us are fearful that the police will come in and beat our pastors and then sentence them to prison terms because they preached the Gospel.

No, we have been blessed and I am thankful for that blessing; but I also recognize that with blessing comes great responsibility.

We have a responsibility to pray- for our brothers and sisters that our bound by prison shackles for their faith.

We have a responsibility to give financially- to provide them with the necessary tools to advance the Kingdom.

We have the responsibility to be involved- Voice of the Martyr's provides a wonderful website to keep you informed of those who are in need. Through their site, you can write letters of encouragement to a brother or sister that is imprisoned for their faith in the Lord Jesus Christ.

You may never physically visit a communist nation or work with the underground church, but you can make a difference with your prayers, financial support, and letters of encouragement.

In Heaven you will have the privilege to meet that brother/sister whom you impacted with your prayers, your love, and your support.

"He is no fool who gives what he cannot keep to gain that which he cannot lose." Jim Elliot

Day Fifty-One

...that at the name of Jesus every knee should bow... and every tongue confess that Jesus Christ is Lord, to the glory of God the Father.

Philippians 2:10,11 NIV

Every year we celebrate a holiday known as the Fourth of July. There are parades and bands play the patriotic songs associated with that particular holiday. We have our hot dogs and apple pie and fireworks light up the night. It is a fun holiday and one that we should never fail to celebrate. Americans proudly display their flags: that red, white, and blue banner of freedom, also known as "Old Glory", and "Stars and Stripes."

There is never a time that I see our flag that I am not moved with love for my country and with gratitude for the men and women that have served so valiantly and selflessly so that you and I can enjoy freedom.

But before the birth of our great nation, Scripture records for us another set of stars and stripes.

Over two thousand years ago, there was a star in the east that led some wise men to a stable where a baby had been born to be the King of the Jews. Matthew 2:4 describes

Jesus' birth and the promise of a Savior, "the One Who would save his people from their sins." He willingly walked the road of shame and suffering so that you and I could walk in freedom.

Isaiah spoke of a Day Star- it is this Star that is the manifested presence of Jesus Christ in the life of every believer. That's you and me.

1 Peter 2:2 reads – "Who Himself bore our sins in His body on the tree, that we, having died to sins, might live for righteousness- by whose stripes you were healed." NKJV

By the very stripes, scourging, and wounds that Jesus took upon Himself; you and I are made completely whole. This truth is in the present tense.

It does not read *might* be healed, *will* be healed, **but** *are* healed.

Jesus paid the ultimate sacrifice so that you and I could live in complete freedom from everything and anything that would try to take us captive and keep us imprisoned.

The wonderful liberty that we enjoy was purchased through the Blood of the Lord Jesus.

Celebrate the country's stars and stripes once a year *but* celebrate the Savior's sacred Stars and Stripes every day- it was His sacrifice at Calvary that gave us our freedom.

Whom the Son sets free is free indeed!

Day Fifty-Two

I am the good shepherd, and know my sheep, and am known by mine.

John 10:14 King James Version

Back in the late seventies, I had the opportunity to spend six weeks with a group of nuns in Channing, Texas. They had been given hundreds of acres of land and had built a Prayer Town. They were busy taking care of the property and one of the responsibilities was taking care of the many sheep they owned. It was during this time that I began to understand the verse for today.

I remember helping the sister that was responsible for the sheep and she told me to call the sheep by name and get them into their pens. So I began to call them: Miriam, John, Peter, Ruth, Mary, etc., (would you expect them to have any other names but Biblical ones) but they would not come to me. The sister that was in charge laughed at my frustration and then she began to call them: Miriam, John, Peter, Ruth, Mary, etc.; as if on cue, they began to march right into their pens.

What was the difference? They knew and recognized her voice. I was a stranger and they would not follow my instructions. I have often heard it said that sheep are dumb but I disagree. They had enough sense to ignore the voice of the stranger and to listen only to the voice of the master.

Jesus is our good Shepherd. Today, He calls you and He reminds you that you are His sheep and that you know His voice. Don't be misled by the voices that clamor for your attention. Don't fall for their deceptions.

You know His voice and He knows yours.

Day Fifty-Three

…I am coming again and I will take you along with Me, so that where I AM you would also be.

John 14:3 Power N.T.

Do you get excited when you are anticipating a celebration? A birthday, an anniversary, Christmas, a wedding? All these celebrations get us in a state of frenzy as we prepare to make everything perfect for that occasion. Brides spend months preparing for that wedding day and in a matter of hours, the festivities are over. Suddenly the guests are gone, wedding cake has disappeared and the marriage has begun. We as believers spend our time preparing for that day: we prepare our hearts for His presence and we work for His Kingdom. We share the Good News with others that they too, might have a part in the eternal festivities. The joys of holidays and special occasions come and go but on that glorious day- we will begin our eternal celebration and we shall see Him face to face!

That is the day that I anticipate- the day when the trumpet shall sound and those who are in Christ will be caught away. I believe that Jesus is as excited about coming for you and me as we are about His return. His celebration will not be for an evening, but it will be for eternity.

Jesus has promised to return and I know that He is true to His word. He is coming back for a victorious church, an overcoming church. He is coming back for you soon!

Are you anticipating His return?

Day Fifty-Four

So remember where you were before you fell. Change your
hearts and do what you did at first.

Revelation 2:5 New Century Version

When you look at the lives of Abraham and Lot, you get the impression that both are spiritual men; until you really look and then you see the differences in their lives.

Abraham lived for God.

Lot lived for self.

Abraham walked in the Spirit.

Lot walked in the flesh.

Abraham walked by faith.

Lot walked by sight.

Abraham walked with God.

Lot walked with Abraham.

Abraham had a very special relationship with God but Lot had a half-hearted commitment to the Lord. He was a spiritual drain on Abram. In chapter 12 of Genesis, God had told Abram, "Leave your country, your relatives, and your father's family, and go the land I will show you."

Abram obeyed and left Haran and Lot went with him. Abram seemed reluctant to part ways with Lot.

When a famine came to the land, Abram went to Egypt (his plan not God's) and he realized that he had actually taken a step backwards and left Egypt.

Unfortunately, it was while in Egypt that Hagar became Sarah's servant. Later, Abraham had a child with her. Ishmael's descendants and Isaac's descendants have been in conflict and even to this day, that terrible conflict remains.

Are there any areas of compromise in your life? Is there a relationship that is draining your spiritual energy? Are there any ungodly influences in your life?

Make a change- determine to give God first place.

Day Fifty-Five

So the King gave the order, and they brought Daniel and
threw him into the lion's den. The King said to Daniel,
"May your God, whom you serve continually, rescue you!"

Daniel 6:16 NIV

Daniel had great favor with the King. He was one of the governor's
who ruled in the King's Kingdom and he was soon to be placed in
charge over the entire kingdom. This brought about much jealousy. It
was not long before the other governors and supervisors were trying to
find a way to get Daniel removed from his position of authority. Never-
theless, they could not find fault because Daniel was hard working and
honest. It did not take them long to realize that the only way to bring
an accusation against him would be concerning the law of his God.

You know the story; they came up with this great plan that for thirty
days no one should pray to any god or human except the king. Disobedience to this new law would result in being thrown into the lion's
den.

Daniel knew about the new law but still he prayed three times a day,
thanking God, just as he had always done.

It wasn't long before the King was informed of Daniel's disobedience.
The King was upset because he loved Daniel and wanted to save him.

It is interesting to me that God did not save Daniel from the den *but* He gave him his deliverance in the den. Daniel could have argued with the King and spoken of the injustice that was being done to him. But Daniel chose to trust His God.

You and I are often in that same predicament. It may not be a literal den of lions we are facing but the circumstances can be just as crushing.

Often when we find ourselves in these dilemmas, we want God to deliver us from the situations. We want to be rescued and we want to be rescued now.

But sometimes the rescue does not come before the deliverance but in the deliverance. It is often in those difficult situations that we learn the most valuable lessons of life. It is often in those situations that we are made the strongest.

I will not ask to be delivered before I have learned my lesson, but I will ask to be made strong that I may endure. I will trust God for just as He was faithful to Daniel- He will be faithful to you and me.

Often times God demonstrates His faithfulness in adversity by providing for us what we need to survive. He does not change our painful circumstances. He sustains us through them.

Charles Stanley

Day Fifty-Six

Therefore the Lord Himself will give you a sign, Behold,
the virgin shall conceive and bear a Son, and she shall call
His name Immanuel.

Isaiah 7:14 NKJV

Immanuel- God with us. What would move God to send His Son
to dwell among us? YOU and ME. You and I have been on his heart
forever and He chose to live among us so that we could live with Him
in heaven.

Jesus was God and He was man. He experienced life just like you and
me. He knew what it was to feel hungry, thirsty, tired, angry, sleepy,
joyful, frustrated, rejected and all the other emotions that exist within
the human heart and soul. But He never sinned. He was perfect.

I remember receiving an e-mail sometime ago and it had all these wonderful pictures of Jesus with children, but what caught my attention,
was that each picture showed him laughing. They were so real that it
was as if I could really hear his laughter. I think that sometimes we forget that He had emotions and that He wasn't this intense looking man
walking around with a grim look on his face.

Jesus knew how to laugh and He knew how to cry.

He knew how to have compassion and He knew how to show correction.

He knew how to celebrate and He knew how to grieve.

In our times of sorrow and pain, we are usually quick to run to him, but do we include him in our times of joy and celebration?

Jesus wants to be Immanuel in your life- God with us: God with you. He wants to be involved in your everyday life. The days that are filled with joy, the days that are routine, the days that are weary, the days that are painful, the days that are sad, the days that are mundane, regardless of your day, He wants to be Immanuel.

Day Fifty-Seven

For unto us a Child is born, Unto us a Son is given; And
the government will be upon His shoulder. And His Name
will be called Wonderful, Counselor, Mighty God, Everlasting Father, Prince of Peace.

Isaiah 9:6 NKJV

Have you ever thought about what the true picture of Christmas looks
like? I have often wondered about what it must have been like in heav-
en on the day that Jesus was born in that stable. I picture angels watch-
ing with anticipation as the darling of heaven comes to earth as a baby.
What about the Father? The emotions that must have been in His heart
as He watched the birth of His Son because He knew that the journey
that started at that stable would end on a cross at Calvary.

I envision the manger with a shadow of the cross looming over it. Beth-
lehem's road led to Calvary.

Jesus' ultimate purpose in coming was to die for your sins and mine.
He died so that we could live. He came to be your savior and to be my
savior.

So many times during the Christmas season, we forget to include the
Savior. Christmas isn't Christmas if Christ is left out. We get caught up
in the shopping, lights, and all the other things that make the season

so special but if we forget Him then all we have done is have a celebration.

Jesus came to reveal the Father to us and He demonstrated His love to us while we were still sinners. He came to preach a message like none other- a message of hope, love, joy, peace, and salvation.

Celebrate Christmas every day. Give Him the gift of your time, your talents and your treasures.

Day Fifty-Eight

Do not speak against one another, brethren.

James 4:11 NASB

Have you ever noticed how easy it is to point out someone's faults and to see their shortcomings?

It is so much easier to gossip about them than to encourage them. Perhaps it is because it makes us feel better about ourselves; after all, I'm not as bad as that person and I'm not doing those things. But the reality is that it is sin- we know it is, but we still do it.

I remember reading an article once about a gentleman that had come up with a formula to combat the problem of gossip and negative speech in his church: T.H.I.N.K.

T- Is it truthful?

H- Is it helpful?

I-Is it inspiring?

N-Is it necessary?

K-Is it kind?

Apply this formula to your life and notice the difference- I should warn you that you may not have as many people with which to converse. What would happen if every church in America followed this simple formula? We might have a genuine revival.

We need to pay attention to the words we are speaking into the lives of others. Are we gossiping and slandering or are we building each other up in the Lord?

If this is an area of struggle for you, ask the Lord to soften your heart and to help you T.H.I.N.K. before you speak.

God, You shut the mouths of the lions in Daniel's den. Shut our mouths when we don't need to speak.

Day Fifty-Nine

A good tree can't produce bad fruit, and a bad tree can't produce good fruit. So every tree that does not produce good fruit is chopped down and thrown into the fire. Yes, just as you can identify a tree by its fruit, so you can identify people by their actions.

Matthew 7:18-20 NLT

Today, there are many who say "I am a Christian" but engage in premarital sex. "I am a Christian" but I get drunk. "I am a Christian" but I cannot tell the truth. "I am a Christian" but I am jealous and envious of others.

To be a follower of Christ (Christian) means much more than saying "I am a Christian." Being a Christian is about having a change, a real genuine change- God's way- a transformation of the heart.

Does this mean that Christians don't sin? Of course not. Christians sin and they slip up but the difference is that there is a genuine repentance. They are willing to acknowledge "I have sinned." A person who continues to live in a continual, habitual, willful state of sin has not yet experienced a transformation. The change ought to be evident to those who know you.

Having Jesus in our lives is more than having the assurance that we won't spend eternity in hell. He wants to guide us and lead us. He wants to fill us with His joy and peace.

Jesus Christ wants to be involved in your life. He wants to walk with you as you go through the day. He wants to be Lord in every aspect of your life.

He wants to be the Lord of your family, your career, your business, your relationships, your social time- He wants to be LORD of all!

He wants to go into the classroom with you. He wants to join you out on the golf course. He wants to go to lunch with you. He wants to go with you on that doctor's visit. He wants to sit with you in that hospital room. He wants to go with you when the boss calls you into his office.

Do you get it? He wants to be Lord of every part of your life!

If He is not Lord of all then He is not Lord at all!

Day Sixty

For God so greatly loved and dearly prized the world that
He (even) gave up His only begotten (unique) Son, so that
whoever believes in (trusts in, clings to, relies on) Him shall
not perish (come to destruction, be lost)but have eternal
(everlasting) life.

John 3:16 Amplified

This is probably one of the most memorized verses of the Bible. It certainly is one that gives us the clearest picture of God's love.

What an incredible picture of God the Savior and man the believer. All we have to do is take God at His word and believe and we enter into a relationship with Him that will forever change us.

When we are saved (born again) we still have the sin nature in us. The sin nature exists because the flesh and soul are being changed day by day. However, the Holy Spirit in us helps us to learn to walk.

Compare this walk to a newborn- can that baby walk or talk? Can he feed himself or change his diaper? No, God gave that baby parents that will nourish and provide and will love unconditionally. They know that someday that baby will be able to take care of its own needs. The Holy Spirit knows that temptation will rear its ugly head and He comes to our aid. He helps us to grow and knows that every day we become more like Jesus.

No one had a choice about being born the first time but the second birth only happens- if you choose. At the cross- the work was God's- now it's up to you to make the choice and let Him be the Lord of your life.

God so loved_ (your name)_ that He gave His one and only Son, that whoever believes in Him shall not perish but have eternal life.

How about you- have you made that choice?

Are you in the "whosoever will" camp?

His love for us is unconditional and He is well aware of yours and my shortcomings and weaknesses, but He still beckons us to come and be a part of His family.

Ask Him to be Lord and Savior and then watch Him change you and your world.